S0-BNT-534

KNOW-IT-ALL

Snakes!

Written by **Christopher Nicholas**

Illustrated by **Mike Maydak**

Reviewed by **Dr. John Behler**, Curator of Herpetology at the Bronx Zoo

Learning Horizons®

AN AMERICAN GREETINGS COMPANY

©2001 Manufactured for Learning Horizons, Inc.
One American Road, Cleveland, OH 44144.
Audio produced by Rick Sellers and Wes McCraw at Creekside Audio
Books made in China. Audio CD made in Hong Kong.
Livres fabriqués en Chine. DC audio fabriqués aux Hong Kong.
©2001 Learning Horizons, Inc.
Visit us at: www.learninghorizons.com

Some are as short as a pencil. Others are as long as a telephone pole! There are almost 3,000 different kinds of them in the world. And even though most are harmless, many people are afraid of them.

What are they?

(Hint: turn the page to find out...)

WHAT IS A SNAKE?

It is a reptile! So are lizards, turtles, alligators, and crocodiles. Snakes are cold-blooded. Their body temperature depends on the temperature of the environment around them. (People are warm-blooded. Our body temperature stays at about 98.6°F (37°C) no matter where we are!)

Snakes often bask in the sun to warm themselves up, then hide in the shade to cool off.

A snake's body is covered with hard little plates called **scales**. It may look wet and slimy, but it is actually dry.

Scarlet Kingsnake

Snakes don't have legs—so they can't walk! They have to glide on their bellies, or move their bodies from side to side, to get where they want to go.

Snakes have two eyes. But they don't have eyelids—so they can't blink! Many snakes can see very well.

Rattlesnake

They don't have ears, but snakes "hear" by feeling vibrations as they slither across the ground. And they can smell with the help of their forked tongue!

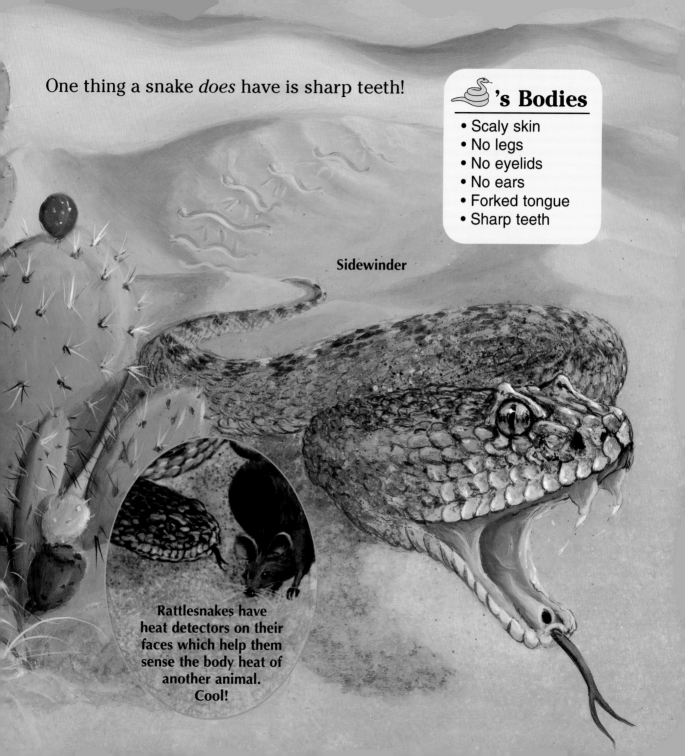

One thing a snake *does* have is sharp teeth!

🐍's Bodies
- Scaly skin
- No legs
- No eyelids
- No ears
- Forked tongue
- Sharp teeth

Sidewinder

Rattlesnakes have heat detectors on their faces which help them sense the body heat of another animal. Cool!

WHERE DO SNAKES LIVE?

Eastern Ribbon Snake

All over the world! But they especially like to be where it is warm. Snakes can be found in jungles, deserts, swamps, and forests. Sometimes they are even in your own backyard!

Green Mamba

They climb through t trees . . . hide in grass a among rocks . . .

Sidewinder

and glide across the sand.

Some even swim in oceans, lakes, and rivers!

Banded Sea Snake

🐍's Live In...
- Jungles
- Deserts
- Swamps
- Forests
- Grass, rocks, trees, and sand
- Oceans, lakes, rivers
- Underground

At the approach of the cold season, some snakes find a hole or den to sleep in until it becomes warm again.

WHAT DO SNAKES EAT?

They eat meat! That's why they are called **carnivores**—a big word that means meat-eaters.

Copperhead

Most snakes feed on small animals. But larger snakes can eat big animals!

Mexican Milk Snake

 **'s Eat**

- Insects and worms
- Frogs and lizards
- Mice, rats, and rabbits
- Birds
- Larger animals
- Other snakes

Some snakes
eat other snakes!

HOW DO SNAKES CATCH AND KILL THEIR FOOD?

Asp Viper

Snakes are sneaky! Sometimes they hide and wait for a meal to pass by. Other times they creep up on an animal—and attack with their sharp teeth! Some snakes use their big, hollow fangs to give victims a shot of deadly venom.

One kind of cobra can blind animals by spitting venom into their eyes.

Cobra

Some snakes use their big, strong bodies to **SQUEEZE** the life out of an animal. This is called **constriction**.

How 's Get Food

- Sharp teeth
- Poison
- Constriction

Emerald Tree Boa

It's kind of like when your aunt comes to visit—and gives you a killer hug!

HOW DO SNAKES EAT AND DIGEST THEIR FOOD?

They always swallow a meal whole—sometimes while it is still alive!

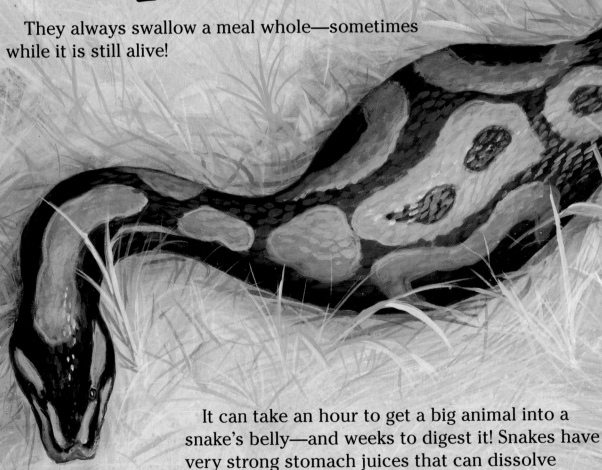

It can take an hour to get a big animal into a snake's belly—and weeks to digest it! Snakes have very strong stomach juices that can dissolve even bones and teeth.

🐍's Eating and Digestion

- Swallow meals whole
- Use specially hinged, wide-opening jaws
- Have strong stomach juices

Ball Python

With its specially hinged jaws, a snake can swallow animals larger than its own head!

HOW DO SNAKES PROTECT THEMSELVES?

Any way they can! Snakes are great hunters—but sometimes they get hunted themselves. Large birds, crocodiles, and other animals love a tasty snake snack.

Sand Viper

Some hide by blending into their surroundings. This is called **camouflage**. Others are brightly colored to warn predators that they may be venomous!

Coral Snake

The rattlesnake will hiss loudly and rattle its tail to frighten enemies.

Rattlesnake

Rubber Boa

How 🐍's Protect Themselves

- Camouflage
- Bright warning colors
- Frightening sounds
- Curling up
- Playing dead
- Moving quickly

The rubber boa curls into a ball and hides its head if attacked.

Black Mamba

The black mamba moves as fast as 7 miles (11 km) per hour to escape predators.

Hognose Snake

d the hognose snake rolls over and plays dead!

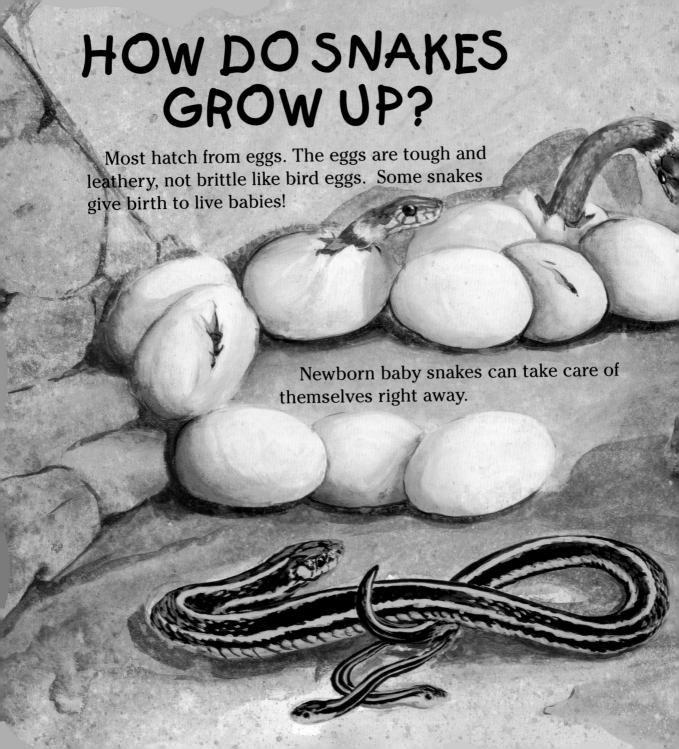

HOW DO SNAKES GROW UP?

Most hatch from eggs. The eggs are tough and leathery, not brittle like bird eggs. Some snakes give birth to live babies!

Newborn baby snakes can take care of themselves right away.

How 🐍's Grow Up

- May hatch from eggs or be born live
- Can care for themselves from birth
- Shed skin

And just as you outgrow your clothes, snakes get too big for their scaly skins. Several times a year they have to **shed**, or peel their skin off. It comes off in one piece—just like a sock!

BET YOU DIDN'T KNOW...

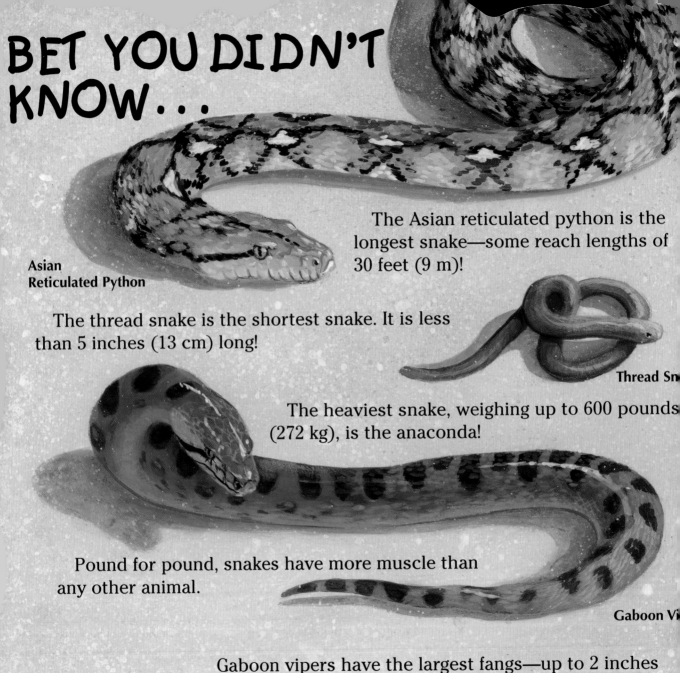

Asian Reticulated Python

The Asian reticulated python is the longest snake—some reach lengths of 30 feet (9 m)!

The thread snake is the shortest snake. It is less than 5 inches (13 cm) long!

Thread Sn

The heaviest snake, weighing up to 600 pounds (272 kg), is the anaconda!

Pound for pound, snakes have more muscle than any other animal.

Gaboon Vi

Gaboon vipers have the largest fangs—up to 2 inches (5 cm) long!

Sometimes snakes are born with two heads!

The Indonesian flying snake can glide through the air from tree to tree.

The African rock python can live up to 2 years without eating.

We have 12 pairs of ribs; snakes have over 200 pairs!

African Rock Python

Rough Green Snake

Long, skinny snakes have only one working lung— they don't have room for two!

DO SNAKES MAKE GOOD PETS?

It depends on you and your family. But a few of these animals—garter, king, and corn snakes, for example—are easy to keep. And, if treated properly, they can become one of the most interesting pets you'll ever own!